HARTFELT POETRY

David Harding

**Dedicated to my children
Paula and Ashley**

ARTHUR H. STOCKWELL LTD
Torrs Park   Ilfracombe   Devon
Established 1898
www.ahstockwell.co.uk

British Library Cataloguing-in-Publication Data.
A catalogue record for this book is available
from the British Library.

ISBN 978-0-7223-4037-0
Printed in Great Britain by
Arthur H. Stockwell Ltd
Torrs Park   Ilfracombe
Devon

Contents

Hartfelt

Knot beeing gude whith werds
Iss know reson knot two rite powitree
Four powitree cums frum thee hart.

Friendship Is for Ever

Relationships with relatives are relative.
That's relative to relationships with friends.
If relatives developed closer friendships,
There would be relatively fewer ends.

The purpose of this muse, relatively speaking,
For those of us who need to live apart,
Is: rebuild your relationships on friendship.
Knowing friendship is for ever helps you start.

Garden Psyche

Passive sexual propagation.
No emotional expectation.
Ever changing repetition
Demonstrating nature's plan.

Giving pleasure through seduction,
With emotional satisfaction.
Comfort in the repetition;
Comprehension of the plan.

Active sexual competition,
And emotional expectation.
Comfort for the human psyche
Through acceptance of the plan.

GBS

If we tread the paths that Shaw trod
In the fields of Hertfordshire,
And we're quietly perceptive,
Luck, we glimpse the herds of deer.

May we chance some other insight
That he had along the way?
If we're quietly perceptive,
Will our thoughts begin to stray?

Did that man tread lonely pathways
Down which only he could veer?
Or can we all seek inspiration
In the fields of Hertfordshire?

Hertfordshire Water Tower

Undulating fields of seedlings
Carpeting the ground before,
Glistening facets showing houses
Underneath a water store.

Reservoir of crystal water
Shining out upon the town,
Stabilising our resources,
Trusting none to let us down.

Cultivating nature's contours,
Adding to her given seed;
We have harnessed more than water
Satisfying human need.

Living proof of our achievements,
Complemented by our hand;
Happiness in rural England,
Glory in our fertile land.

Redundancy

Telling the family,
Nowhere to hide.
Internal panic,
External pride.

Financial problems,
Paperwork guide.
Internal panic,
External pride.

Job search beginning,
All classified.
Internal panic,
External pride.

Leaving the company,
Cheque on the side.
Internal panic,
External pride.

Social security,
Queuing inside.
Internal panic,
External pride.

New life beginning,
No suicide.
Internal calmness,
External pride.

Time it has passed now,
Quite satisfied.
External calmness,
Internal pride.

Our September Sadness
Dedicated to Peggy

Another day unfolding
And no one yet is dead.
Holidays are paid for
And there's happiness ahead.

Aircraft, charged and ready,
Prepare to lift and fly
Their unsuspected flight path
That ensured three thousand die.

* * * * *

And in some quite corner
Two autumn lovers plan
Their measured small diversion,
As only lovers can.

No man-made deadly agent,
Just nature's power unleashed;
And with her mighty hammer
Another life deceased.

To brutalise and batter
Her selection of sweet kinds,
Fate needs no intervention
From fanatics' twisted minds.

Sore – See – Saw

I saw the hedge at Mother's house,
An eyesore overgrown.
I saw and sawed till I was sore,
And now the birds have flown.

I saw them soar away that day
And wished they would return.
My arms were sore, my heart was sore.
The hedge I saw their home no more.

Stress

Do I believe that what I am feeling
Is really a feeling of feeling stress,
Or am I just feeling a feeling of feeling
And what I am feeling is merely distress?

Who do I turn to, to talk through the feeling –
The panic of feeling my lack of control?
Will I admit to others to feeling
That stress is really taking its toll?

Should I, then, leave the solution to later
When distress has abated and my feeling is good?
Though I feel that this answer is lacking conviction
And I need to confirm that I'm quite understood.

My feeling is real and should be debated,
For I need to resolve the panic I feel.
And to leave it to later may open the question –
Will I be able to describe the ordeal?

I may not be ready to talk on the subject;
Somebody needs to be talking to me!
For I am unable to decide on the timing
When feeling this feeling, whate'er it may be.

Do I believe that what I am feeling
Is really a feeling of feeling stress,
Or am I just feeling a feeling of feeling
And what I am feeling is merely distress?

I may not . . .
Help!

That Smile

Introspective journey.
Striving to stay awake.
Drab, dank day of giving,
With supermarket break.

Coke-and-sandwich purchase,
Young lady loading car.
I stand, controlled and waiting,
Bag and baggage bar.

Turning from her labour,
She finds me waiting there.
Silently she thanks me;
Smiles through tangled hair.

Platonic, sensual contact.
A meeting in the rain
Rekindled choked-back memories
Of life's potential gain.

The Garden Labourer

Not for him the words were written
By the scholars of the past.
Tutored by the God that made him,
Strong in arm and strength to last.

Weathered by the changing seasons,
Elements of sun and rain.
He could face them without bother –
Muscled back accepting pain.

Paper plans, strategic thinking
On their own were not enough.
Labourer with skilful talents
Some mistook as vaguely rough.

Asking little of his lifestyle,
Always there to do the toil.
He it was who fashioned mountains,
Dug the lakes and moved the soil.

The Oak Tree

Rooted high upon the landscape
Stands the steadfast oak on guard,
Holding back her summer secrets
In a winter-wand facade.

Camouflaged, a thousand starlings
Exploding forth as wings unfold;
Mystery and inner knowledge –
What other secrets does she hold?

War and want and exploitation,
Love and lust and jubilation –
All are sensed by twigs and branches,
Stored and logged by unknown sources.

Would we had the sensibility
To tap that mighty book of history.
Leafing through the layered pages
Ringed and researched down the ages.

Catalogued for contemplation,
Lines of literature on file.
Documented facts to ponder,
Penned and paragraphed in style.

Open then to all who wish to
See the truth of what occurred.
Yet, might it be more to your liking
If Madam Oak had not observed?

Walking

Head and shoulders,
Arms and torso,
Gliding on alternate legs.
Plan the journey,
Sight the milestones,
Gliding on alternate legs.

See the beauty,
Sense the unknown,
Striding on alternate legs.
Shoulders high and
Torso straining,
Striding on alternate legs.

Distance covered,
Time is passing,
Trudging on alternate legs.
Shoulders aching,
Torso paining,
Trudging on alternate legs.

Meditating
On the journey,
Lifting forth alternate legs.
Feel contentment
At achievement
Of those alternating legs.

Wind Pump

Wind pump winding by the river –
Wonder why it winds away?
Drinking up the sodden marshlands,
Sending water on its way.

Why did people tend the lowlands
When the highlands were nearby?
What was it they toiled and worked for
Underneath that troubled sky?

Driven by some inner challenge;
Seduction by the peaceful fen.
Shying from the crowded places,
Solitude from other men.

Mastering the ebb and flow, their
Stubbornness achieved the feat.
Bringing forth the latent bounty
Hidden there amongst the peat.

Work

Drive the journey to the network.
Target the vision; culture the action.
Train the instincts to assumption.
Known and unknown, that's the challenge.

Why we do it, that's the question.
Exercise of brain and muscle.
Is it likely that we need to
Play the role expected of us?

Could it be that we invented
The directing that we needed
To fulfil some innate mission,
Set to show our differential
From the more successful species
That we live with on this planet?

Young Love

Bright eternity,
Opaque tomorrow.
Emotional oscillation,
Panic and tranquillity.

Your Dream

When plans lose direction,
When people seem less keen,
When you are feeling doubtful,
Just hang on to your dream.

Your dream is oh, so special,
And deserves to be upheld.
Ideas are hard to come by,
Are so easily dispelled.

We need to take direction,
To understand what's seen
By those who have the vision,
So hang on to your dream.